THE

OBSERVER

THE
OBSERVER

Daniel Craig Toney

gingersnapbooks
Murfreesboro, TN

Cover art by: Daniel Craig Toney

www.danielcraigtoney.com

ISBN 10: 0-9796328-1-1
ISBN 13: 978-0-9796328-1-5

Library of Congress Control Number: 2007937142

Library of Congress Subject Headings
1. Poetry

Published by: g i n g e r s n a p b o o k s
(An imprint of Artistic Spaces Publishing)
           P.O. Box 330703
           Murfreesboro, TN 37133-0703

Printed in the United States of America

Dedicated to: Our Father

OBSERVATIONS

THE OBSERVER

It takes time to become the one
To listen, but to stay apart
The all trained observer
The one without a care, or a heart

I can't say when or why
I became the one, who, on the side
Put together all the secrets
Who'd listen and become the guide

I always knew to pay a mind
To what would come to be
To listen to the chosen ones
Without wallowing in debris

To begin the process took a knack
And sometimes touched a nerve
But no matter where or how I began
I was brought here to observe.

SATURDAY MORNING BACKPACK

Seems you've made all the right preparations
To help you on your way
You've brought your favorite backpack with the focus
of the day
As you discuss the paths you'll take
And directions from your guide
You trust his compass settings now
As if he would be there by your side

Your guide has mapped his own life
He follows it today
He learned it from another past
Whose hair has since turned grey
You know that if you listen well
And never go astray
You'll hit the rainbow's end, my friend
At happenings' doorway

So don't veer off in another direction
When you know which path to take
There've been times you did, you know
And you recall that fate
Listen well and don't forget
Directions that you hear
For many times await your choice
Some you'll hold quiet dear

Don't falter onto another course
Because inside your heart

You know your guide looks out for you
He'd done it from the start
He wants for you the very best
You know he's got that knack
All along he wishes you
Could take his own backpack.

BREAKFAST BETWEEN FRIENDS

They come together from different worlds
Each coming for to be
The understanding listener
That the other needs

They found each other long ago
In a world far, far away
That existed for a time
In that place called yesterday

They listened, formed a bond
Decided to impart
Their wisdom one to the other
In the matters of the heart

They would listen to unfolding stories
As told first hand from deep
And within the heart and soul it poured
The secrets sworn to keep

Make sure you listen carefully
The next time could be you
And not only hear, but listen
Or the meaning you'll misconstrue.

HONEST OBSESSION

It's an honest obsession, she said with a smile
To have what I've wanted for more than awhile
To take what is needed . . . it isn't a flaunt
To take what I get and get what I want

I just don't get it, how the other half lives
How could they ever be happy? I mean, just
what gives?
And the window shopping just what is it for
To go in, look around, and come out of the store

Who cares what you buy? It's always the deal
To get something for so little, I like to get real
Gather what I want, how can I fail
Whip out the plastic, no need to curtail

And as he listened quietly to all that she said
How could he express to his newlywed
That he had borrowed all she outspent
And now they couldn't even make rent.

THE WISE MAN

The young ones, unknowingly, need the wise man to speak
They need his wisdom now for the times they are weak
You know—but you don't know . . . you reap what you sow
This lesson should have been learned a long time ago

Tomorrow, once again, your fate will arrive
If you prepare wisely you are sure to survive
Because, either way, your day you'll get through
But on your best footing? That part's up to you

Learn knowledge wisely, take care as you do
For all that is spoken is not meant for you
So many leaders speaking their mind
Saying act now don't be left behind

Learn as they speak . . . is it for your own good?
Or will the things they offer turn out as they should
Changing your path to the one that they take
Could map out your course to another mistake

Listen wisely to the one who lightens your load
And takes rocks from your path, helps you through the
crossroad
Keep your spirit safe, but don't lock it away
Feed it and nurture it each and every day

Allow your happiness to come from within
And count on the one on whom you can depend
What's right and wrong doesn't change with the time
Don't take the path that you'll regret a lifetime

Take time to listen to your spirit . . . it's deep inside
It might just help strengthen your from a backslide
Don't let it be poisoned or lead only part way
Always doing what's right never takes you astray

Just like a precious metal. As impurities make it less strong
So shall be your value to help bring you along
Time to heal your body and mind you must set apart
Because you need to take heed from inside your heart

At end . . . some will listen to the words that I say
Some only hear….their roads end in decay
Have faith and believe, always take care
Protect against evil and strive to prepare

Living for yourself is a lonely time it's true
Much wiser to live so your loved ones will be proud of you
And living your life without compromise
Will make sure that you keep your eyes on the prize

Speak not harsh word . . . learn to listen as you should
Thrills last for the moment and don't deliver eternal good
Don't do what is wrong . . . don't push that lever
Stop mistakes before they happen . . . Consequences
last forever.

FRIENDS

Such great friends you claim to be
And no one in their right mind would disagree

Whenever anyone sees you around each other
They can tell it's much more than brother to brother

There is a bond there that can't be denied
You are happiest when you are on the same courtside

You think you are such a close friend
Yet can we ever guess what is yet to impend

And when it comes down to all that you say
Do you scratch the surface by the end of the day

Do you listen and read between the lines
Or want to keep it on the surface, all by design

You actually think you know how he feels
What is in his head—what is actually real

Only listening to what you want to hear
You'll never quiet hold anything dear.

AUGUST SO SOON

The sun moves quickly across the sky
    It keeps moving past
Because it moves for one close to me
    August comes too fast

I gather up my papers, I need to go
    And the morning turns to noon
And echoes for those who know
    That it ends too soon

Speak your heart to those held close
    And listen 'fore close to noon
And summer keys a parting note
    And August ends too soon

Does December loom within our touch
    Can we reach beyond it's grasp
Because it's but August, this we feel
    And August might not last

So just because you don't care
    How quickly your day moves
Please keep my friend in mind
    As I try to make the day last.

The Observer

KEEPSAKE

I know you look familiar
Though I know we've never met
The face is so distinctive
It's one I wouldn't forget

So that's why you find me standing still
Stunned with all your grace
Seeing you in front of me
Has set me in my place

I don't know where I should start
What you'd like to hear me say
It's been a long time coming
But I've so looked for this day

I see you are a treasure
Entrusted to us here
We've been waiting so patiently
For the better part of a year

None of us know the paths you'll choose
As you set upon your way
We only know that you'll take with you
The traits we've passed this day

I'll pray daily for your needs
And the directions that you'll take
May you use what I pass to you
Then pass along your own keepsake.

HINDSIGHT

Waiting
Anticipating you
Tomorrow seemed bright
As I sat there, start of moonlight

I heard the rain against the back window
And it splattered as it began to flow
Like the atmosphere
Trying to hold back a pool of tears

And then the avalanche began to grow
Though only against the back window
The tears washed away time
As I sat there trying to unwind

My front glass was yet dry
Although there was no clear sky
The overhang of protection kept the rain away
And I know I wanted to protect you that way

The doors to the hospital opened wide
To release my candy-striper kept inside
Moving out, rain hit the windshield
The wipers wiped so we didn't have to yield

I know that I listened well that night
To the words inside my head in the dim light
Not sure why they stuck to this day
Like these words were caught in some passageway.

The Observer

TOMORROW NEVER KNOWS

Listen, Dad, oh won't you please
To all that's said today
Because tomorrow may not be
It might just go away

Or daughter, maybe you
Should be the one to say
What is really on your heart
So it won't fade away

You see tomorrow never knows
Just who's smile to bless
Some wake up, while others sleep
While others, yet regress

Next time when you don't listen
As someone speaks their mind
What they say might linger
Longer than them, you find

Because as hearts are spoken
With words we won't outgrow
Sometimes fall on deaf ears
Yet tomorrow never knows.

The Observer

As Wine is to Life

As the sun comes out of the ocean
And I find myself gazing at the shoreline
The thoughts that fill my head
Focus on a vintage bottle of wine.

The grapes are blessed in the vineyard
The vineyard blessed by the sunshine
But one thing here is very clear
I still focus on that bottle of wine

As the time comes to pick the grapes
To make something special and fine
The long maturing process comes next
Evolving into that bottle of wine

Grapes face a long road of nurturing
And patience while growing on the vine
Once they are picked come the preparation
That goes into making that bottle of wine

In our lives we grow with choices we make
Through each rise and following decline
We get more understanding
As we make our own bottle of wine.

The Observer

CAVE

Deep
Within the catacombs
Lies the crevices of darkness
Dank and recessed
Away
Unreachable
The cobwebs
That make your attempts to understand

Reservoir
And from within
A spring
Bringing life
Giving hope
A meandering thought
To be fostered
And to be fed
   . . . not to be squelched.

My Father's Son

What I have always been
And truly have become
Can all be summed up in 5 words
I am my father's son

And though my path diverges
And I'm way past twenty-one
There's not been a time I wasn't proud
To be my father's son

And if I got to choose today
Who I could have set example
I can tell you, bar-none
When push comes to shove
And actions turn to love
I'm glad I'm my father's son.

The Observer

OTHER SIDE OF MIDNIGHT

There is the other side of midnight
Few know, yet fewer find
For just because you are here
Doesn't mean you see the sign

You came here searching for yourself
You hear it call your name
It stopped calling long ago
But you listen all the same

Better to heed the new call you know
To a real life, apart from pretend
One that will last beyond today
With promises you can depend

As things fall due (as things tend to do)
Heart, health, eternal happiness, bills
All call and a deaf ear makes no difference
Tomorrow waits not, mistakes to think it will

There is a sign for all to read
Found the other side of midnight
Whether or not you heed the signs
You know there is no sunlight

And you became lost, with no searchlight
That willpower was not your own
You found yourself pulled into that other world
That in time, you've outgrown

The Observer

You find yourself now, stronger,
As strong as you want to be
Chose to be weak, you know that fate
Nice to be past that destiny.

The Observer

SHOW THE WAY

I don't ever have to ask what was right
Or what was wrong
I just came to know it well
And know it all along

And in the heat of problem moments
When I was able to stay calm
I know that deep inside me
I can thank my mom

In life I knew that sometimes
Rough has followed through
And times have come along
When I thought I had enough

But I seem to persevere
And stand about the pile
To make sure I keep the upper hand
And face it with a smile

I owe you both so very much
I never could repay
You've always been the very light
At the top of the stairway

The promise you place in me
I never could fulfill
The light that shows my way each day
The light that always will

You've planted seeds of hope
And seeds that show the start
And seeds of kindness, faith and dreams
I keep inside my heart

I could go on and on
But think it's time to close
What I am, I owe you both
Everybody knows.

Indifferent Attitude

Go ahead and speak your mind
I'll hear as speak you must
Just don't expect me to reiterate
As your words they gather dust

Setting here across the gap
That spreads 'tween the two of us
Saying words we come to say
Yet feelings aren't discussed

You go your way and I'll go mine
That seems to be the norm
We do what's expected
As we so try to conform

So speak to me of what you will
And I will do the same
But if we get defensive
We'll forget just why we came

To hear, but not to listen
Lest we take it to our heart
And be hurt or get defensive
Get the horse before the cart

And so we spend another day
Getting just a crumb
Of what is going on
And striving for the numb

Coping makes a course of it's own
Of this I am quiet sure
We are all striving for someway
In which we can endure

It isn't always what is done
The charts that sand of time
But what we leave undone
That stops the "us" from rhyme.

HAPPY INSIDE

I guess that you are happy
I mean, why else would you laugh
Yet your smile seems so hidden
Caught in a photograph
And you say the right line
'cause you know what I need to hear
But the words somehow fall short
And never come near

I know it isn't in your heart
I don't know how I know
Getting what, where, and how you need
And I get the overflow
You've become someone else
Once you came to stay
I sometimes feel so turned around
I almost feel betrayed

Laughter interrupts my night
I wake up to your smile
I stay because it's how I am
For now, it's my style
I think you'll be happy
And you'll get what you need
I hope I can get what I want, too
If we are to succeed.

The Observer

TELL ME, AGAIN

Tell me again why I should care
And what it is that we share
You're only happy when I'm under your thumb
For me to be happy I need to be numb
Why do you think I should jump when you call
Do you think I have no sense at all
I'm living in a state of despair
Come and go as you want—unfair

Tell me, if you can, just what we've become
And why I should wait for you to throw me a crumb
When I feel the need to retreat
Because it's just another defeat
Of past unbalance and despair
So it is and leave us where
Talking and listening to ourselves
Place our thoughts back on their shelves

Because we know we only hear
What we tend to hold quiet dear
Like a worn out phrase in a forgotten song
That tends to ramble on far too long
Singing notes that no longer blend
We can tell we've come to our end
Singing words once held so dear
I can no longer sing them without a tear
Goodbye.

The Observer

IN THE END

And just the way you wanted me to be
I became a different man
Living by your rules became the norm
And like a child I followed your plan

But I don't know if it worked out
Just the way you planned it to
Because when I thought we reached
The rainbows end, there was no follow-through

And so it's now I come to see
That in trying to build your dreams
When you try to live life thought another's eyes
You grow apart at the seams

So let me say one thing more
No need to pretend
I'm really rather thankful
We reached our bitter end.

FREE

Thanks for setting me free
For helping me to learn to take care of me
For so long I couldn't see
What you had done inside of me

But when you stepped from my view
No longer did I have to be two
I found I no longer had to weigh
The happiness had begun to decay

Seeing how sad I'd become
And seeing I wasn't the only one
only helped me to start to see
That you became the death of me

And when I started to fade away
I couldn't see the light of day
You had caused me to regress
And left me only emptiness

So, thanks for stepping to the side
You shoved me into quite a ride
It wasn't 'til you let me be
That I found the happy me.

The Observer

THOUGHTS, CARES

Thoughts, feelings
Rumblings, reeling

Focus a blur
Direction astir

Redirect
Non detect

Brick on brick
Stick on stick

Build up?
Construct

Take down?
Destruct

Opposite . . . maybe
Can't care, baby

When to stop.

BREAK

All was calm
Before the break
And, as if on cue, it approached
But untrustingly I moved toward it
Unknowingly I called out for it's peril
And the break came
Unforeseen, yet relentless
And that break . . . we became
And were
Face to face
And it occurred to me
What had caused the break
It was set into motion
Step by step process
Started misaligned
And continued to fracture
Until nothing was left to fit.

The Observer

MIRAGE

Sometimes we feel compelled to dwell inside the past
We try to learn from our mistakes and build it all again
We dive into the future as if it just won't last
And see a mirage that isn't real and take it on the chin.

We might even have some help to paint what isn't there
To add to the palate, familiar shades that we find
appealing
Maybe we see a side of ourselves . . . happy, without
a care
Or kicked right back the other way when real gets a
revealing

The room sits still . . . the silence seems loud
Only me to hear . . . listening to the sound
Overhead the ceiling looms and becomes a dark rain cloud
And like a dream when I can't get up . . .
I give up and stay down

So don't see just what you want
Because you just might find
That what you see that's really real
Bites you from behind.

COMPROMISE
(my apologies to Bob Dylan)

Is it difficult for you to realize
That you are all about compromise
As you begin to agonize
Over the present that unfolded from your past

Well I find it hard to surmise
Why you can't seem to rise above the lies
And that is all we can finalize
How can that build something that can ever last?

As the situation you begin to apprise
We see things from another's eyes
With the chaos that grows to jeopardize
The albatross that plays like a rebroadcast

Would it be all that unwise
To accept things as if a reprise
And not to view it with total surprise
When you come up with the same weathercast.

FOUNDATION

How much a foundation can be built on sand?
How true is the feeling I get when I take your hand?
It all comes down to where we draw the line
Between what is felt and what designed

What does it take to misunderstand
When you feel like a bike without a kickstand
Feet kicked out from under you . . . fish on dry land
What does it take to understand

What does it take to misunderstand
What it's a foregone conclusion in the quicksand
When you get a nightmare instead of dreamland
What does it take to finally understand?

THE CHILL

There are so many voices
That I hear across the room
But the sights that greet me there
Leave us lonely and in gloom

Some voices seem to point
To a happier time I assume
But I can't seem to find the words
To take us from our doom

Once the actions seemed to fill the space
We found inside the bedroom
But now the words never seem to fit
The mood that suit's the perfume

Nothing seems to be amiss
Or cause for worry or fret
Open up to me. Don't hide.
They are fine . . . and yet . . .

When the room is full with you and I
And the TV is finally still
The warmth I find from within
Cannot replace the Chill.

Happy Together

I tried to let you know
How happy you made me
I don't know if I succeeded
Couldn't have made you that happy
I asked God to help make you pleased
You deserve so much happiness
For the love you sent my way
Our hearts were so filled with love
They still are to this day
You will always be filling my heart
Wouldn't have it another way
Please welcome me back please do
I want to be together forever . . . I love you.

SONGS

I hear songs differently now
Now they aren't the same
So many things sprung to life
When you first called my name

I felt like only the beginning
Was written for we two
The part about feeling forever
And where or what we'd do

You would hold me in your arms
At the end of every day
All the bad that had me down
Until it went away

Love songs pale in comparison
To what you taught my heart
The devotion, the caring, the sharing, too
That you showed me from the start

You held on, long as you could
It took an angel to be so kind
I didn't know how many songs
Have been written about left behind.

The Observer

AND WHEN THAT DAY COMES

And when that day comes
And I'm by your side
I know the tears will flow
I can't be dry-eyed
I have come to realize
The times I came up short
My misunderstandings
And lack of life support

And when I thought I understood
But I didn't, I've come to know
Must not tried hard enough
That gives me much sorrow
Wish I'd married you sooner
Of that I'm quiet sure
Please forgive my shortcomings
And my being immature

I miss you so much, you know
Wish you were with me
In your arms where I belong
Is where I want to be
Please bless me when my time comes
For us to be together
Because I want to be with you,
Happy together, forever.

I'M TIRED

"I'm tired," she said
I heard with my heart
I knew what she meant
I had from the start
But couldn't accept
What she was trying to say
Please, not now
Maybe some other day

"I'm tired," she said
Yet once again
And if I accepted
My world would cave in
Didn't want her to speak
Or fly away
Needed her there
Needed her to stay

I fought back the tears
I ached down inside
It felt like the roller coaster
Cut short my ride
Things would be better
She again would confide
She didn't understand
I'd rather her by my side

And once the time grew near
I knew I needed to say
To have a place beside her
And it was okay.

The Observer

AUTUMN CAME OVERNIGHT

Autumn came overnight
You knew you would go
The look in your eyes
The lack in your glow
You were findin the gold
At the end of your rainbow
Worrying more for the others
You would leave back below.

Autumn came overnight
As if right on cue
Holding on for us
I had not a clue
Of all that transpired
Of all you went through
To make it easier for us
'Cause you already knew

Autumn came overnight
I want you to know
If I could live my life over
We'd hear the wind blow
Your memories would all be sweet
You'd never have sorrow
Only our happiness
No tears for our tomorrows

So save me a place
Life we talked about
One with sweet happiness

Inside and out
Where we can be blessed
And without a doubt
Hold each other again
Faith will show me the route.

The Observer

BEARS

I got our white bear out
Delivered with love so true
The one from Valentine's Day
With the heart that says "I love you"

You thought I shouldn't have spent so much
I actually spent more
But it was for both of us
I got them from the store

I set them on the bed a week ago
They are looking at me, still
Well, not exactly, just that way
But I'll tell it to you real

The only one looking my way
Is the bear that would be you
It is looking right my way
I tell it to you true

The bear that would be me
Isn't pointing at me at all
It's eyes are on a picture of you
Set against the wall

At two o'clock this morning
I noticed this very thing
As I sit here on our bed
Still wearing my ring

I know, you know it's hard right now
To go on day by day
But I plan to do just that
You'd want it just that way.

The Observer

ANGEL

An angel came to earth
And I'll never be the same
'cause once she touched my life
She began to call my name

She found a place in my heart
And she's in there still
She taught me about true love
What it took to make it real

Her smile could light a room
Her eyes could the same
I was so happy to hear her voice
When she would call my name

She endured so much to stay with me
And stayed long as she could
She thought only of others
And touched our lives for good

I tried to take care of her
God was nice to count on me
And she was good to see it, too
And how I had that need

God helped me to make her happy
And I asked him every day
To guide me and direct me
And help me to find a way

The Observer

My angel touched so many hearts
And brought other angels love
So they might grow up to be strong
And learn about God above

You see not always do you have a say
What gives us all a choice
It was living life the way you did
That made us love you Joyce.

Pain Run Away

Grandma died
Hurt, pain
Deny she was gone
Wouldn't let myself get close to other grandparents
Wouldn't let myself get close
Losses . . . some come back
Some never do . . . but are around
Some never do
When I go I won't be alone
I just need to find the ones gone before
Who I cry for now
Not because I am sad
Just because.

ONE

The silence is deafening
Though I strain so I hear
Each unspoken word
As if you were near

Folding back the sheet for one
Holding back a tear
I guess I miss you way too much
That becomes quiet clear.

PART . . . WHOLE

Yesterday isn't for everyone
Part of me is gone
My tomorrow will never be the same
There is an emptiness inside
I try not to dwell on it but I have no choice
Someday she will be with me again
And once again I will be made whole

I try to fill my thoughts
My today's with anything
I have little choice but to carry on
Joyce will always be the answer to what is missing
I hope I will be a welcomed part
To make her whole . . . when the time comes.

Forgiveness . . . Faith

I've faced true forgiveness
The forgiveness you give yourself is important
But I've faced it from God and I've faced it from some-
one special . . .
Life is not always fair . . . but God is . . .
Sometimes He works in mysterious ways and we don't
understand . . . but far too often we don't try hard
enough to understand . . . and that is the problem
We think we understand so we quit trying to under-
stand more . . . and we miss out on the understanding
that God promised us . . .
Because of our shortchanging our efforts, we end up
shortchanging so much that we didn't know . . . until
it's too late.

FORGET-ME-NOTS

I bought you some flowers and hoped you would see
All of the love inside of me
'cause it had hidden itself from other's view
I meant it for no one other than you

Forget-me-nots from me to you
Some might say they were long overdue
I hope you can look back without being sad
Try to focus on good times we had

I took too long to make you my wife
I hope you know how you've changed my life
Because of you and our love that I knew
I became more inclined to pursue

To find a life though it must be
Without you now and I hope you see
Not sure the flowers I laid to the ground
But forget-me-nots they are 'cause you're
Heaven-bound.

EYE OF THE HURRICANE

Hello, once again
Is it time for all the pain?
Time for it all to sink in
Hit by a moving train

Maybe it's all in vain
I'm not sure what to say
Thoughts, words inside my brain
Life an oft forgotten refrain.

Caught inside a tailspin
Clamber for fresh air
I don't know where to begin
Better not to care

Is there progress deep inside
Maybe to remain
Turning inward to abide
In the eye of the hurricane.

My Focus

Change was inevitable
Now I don't rush home
Focus gets all fuzzy
When I'm going all alone

I still have a house
With a door I find
Where I can go
To lock the world behind

But now I don't have you there
To hold me in your arms
To take away all the pain
To take away all harm

What I felt so deep inside
While you were holding me
The love, the joy, the happiness
I never could conceive

It was the best thing I ever felt
You took away all my stress
And it's why I feel so lucky now
Why I feel so blessed

Eyes for the Future

I see the sparkle in your eyes
That says you are glad to see
The look in mine that says
We were meant to be

How does it feel when the cold winds blow
And I'm not around to stop the chill
That surrounds your heart
Or does the thought of us keep you warm

You came running out of the night
Opened all the right doors
And close the right backdoors
And the future seemed bright

You painted the right picture
In my watercolor dreams
Opening the door for the future
Putting away the past and any pain and screams

It's nice to know we chose the way
Toward our goal and happiness
And we followed the sweet path
So our lifetimes will now be blessed.

MISSED

Quiet is the room
I hear the silence in my mind
It's speaking to me
Repeating the note that I find
I missed you, it said
And then it was signed
Love, Kay
I hope you're not blind

To know that my life changed
The very first day
You came into my life
And now I can say
My love wasn't one
That went only halfway
My love goes deeper
I love you Kay

There once was a time
Before we once met
That I saw myself
As my only asset
But now I can say
Without regret
That I became us
We're a happy duet

When I think of the future
When I think of someday
When, if I let it

My hair will turn gray
We'll keep climbing together
Our life's stairway
You'll always hear
How I love you Kay.

ALL WITHIN YOUR EYES

I fought back what I felt inside
Wall around my heart
Then I think to that smile I saw
And loved from the very start

It lets me know how happy you are
And how I know you care
At those special times I need you most
You make sure you are there

No need to say how you feel
Don't you realize?
It shouldn't be a secret
I should see it in your eyes.

THE MEMORY

When tonight turns into a well lit dawn
Who will be left to carry on?

And in the name of all mankind
Will those, whose verse will be left behind
Be passing along a golden baton
To another,
    Who someday will move on
Or will the chosen
    Fall to uninclined
And thus languish
    Undefined

I ask myself
    For need to know
Someday
    Will be my time to go.

The Observer

WALK OF CLOUDS

Thick and heavy the morning
Hanging sluggishly in midair
No more heavy than the overhanging rain clouds
Of which I am well aware.

But the rain does not come.

Leaves, blown by an October breeze
Fall on the ground where they lay
Lie still in the thick grass
Echoing the mood of the day.

Still, the rain does not come.

Holding to a rail for support
An old man slowly moves up the hill
Like the leaves, he is wrinkled with age
He keeps moving—never still.

The rain does not fall.

One foot after the other
Not noticing each step
Overall goal comes closer
Toward which he crept.

And the clouds yet hold their moisture.

His old shoes drag along the concrete
Scuffing off their life all the while

The Observer

Drifting quietly out of view
Without as much as a smile.

The clouds go unnoticed.

Rays of sunlight find the hill
From behind the silhouette of the gray cloud
No longer is there threat of rain
No longer dismal, darkened, shroud.

And the old man turns to come back down.

His walk becomes more lively
As with each step he seems to cover more ground
His face carries the hint of a grin
He makes his way back toward town.

It becomes overcast once more.

The old man breaks into a smile
That even the clouds can't erase
Walking from the picture
Now gone without a trace.

It begins to sprinkle.

IN THE NIGHT

Wondering alone aimlessly
Through the mist in the wind
Wrapping the fog around you
A whisper says where you've been

The freedom of the night
Is like a cage on the soul
For what can be a diamond
Always starts out as coal

When morning comes
The future you need will unwind
Will the whispers left in the night
Be the ones left behind?

The morning light flickers
Reaching for your face to touch
A tender thought reaches your mind
Before you can think too much

You don't know what thoughts
Should be on your mind
Only "Will the whispers in the night
Be the ones left behind?"

QUESTIONS

What do you think about
When I'm not near?
Does the time seem to move by as quickly
As it does when you are here?
Is the night and day as sweet
Or do you somehow feel incomplete,
When I'm not near,
When you're not here?

Do you think of freedom
And all that you can do?
Do you feel the strength of depending on me
As I depend on you?
Does your laughter come from in your heart
And is your heart filled with my spirit?
Are you thinking of how it leaps
When I'm near it?

Does the feeling go away
That feeling deep inside
The smile that reaches the corners
Of your face
Or does it try to hide from view
And disappear without a trace
When I'm not near
When you're not here?

The Observer

THAT NIGHT

You came running into my arms from out of the night
Opened your mind and opened your heart
A seed was then planted
And grew from the start

Turning away and into the night
We walked away and out of sight

How did it feel when you stepped out the door
After being together on the dance floor
Did you feel the chill of the wind surrounding your heart
Taking over the warmth that we felt from the start

Turning away and into the night
We walked away and out of sight

Now that we find ourselves where we are today
And the path to the future we can see
Do you ever wonder where you would be
If I didn't find you and you didn't find me?

I ASK

I don't mean to crowd you
Or ask too much
Of you . . . your smile
Your loving touch,
Your eyes that see me
Best or worse
Were what drew me closer
They touched me first
What I ask is all that is
Yours to give
And I will do the same
As long as I live.

WALLS

I found my love in time you see
We didn't really try
We allowed ourselves to be
The people we had inside

The walls we built around us
Where we went to hide
Have left us with a bitter taste
Trails of tears we had to cry.

POINT IN TIME

Shine on today, tomorrow
Shine on glorified light
Bring true happiness to me
It all began that night

Someone sweet and kind
Came into my sight
Deep down beneath the surface
So perfect and so right

My stone walls began to tumble
My heart began to melt
All loneliness left behind
The feelings that I felt

They talk about that point in time
When things start to fall into place
I guess that road began
When first I saw your face.

Coming Through

I see it in your eyes
Your smile brings me closer to you
I don't see it when you're not yourself
A look like you're confused
Allow your life to be happy
No need for all your blues
Hold on to each other tightly
We'll pull each other through.

LOVE SCENES

You are filled with beauty
And scenes of deep felt love
Dreams of tomorrow
Under clear skies above
Soaring ever onward
Like a pure white dove

Honey, if you can hear my thoughts
Playing in your mind
Release your heart to me
I know that you will find
The love we have together
Could never be unkind.

THE HIGHWAY

Driving down the highway
Just as fast as I should ride
We're all headed somewhere
Some have pulled off on the side
Some have to do a lot to make sure
Their lives are justified

I've been in and out of life's illusion
Farther than the eye can see
No matter how far I went
I could never get away from me
But now as my life unfolds
I'm now who I want to be.

LOST FEELINGS

Feelings—so far removed for so long
It's hard to say for sure
Am I hearing fear of hurt and pain
Or a cry for help behind the door
There's a fire beneath
Where the heart runs deep
And fear is washed ashore
There's a distant deep loneliness trying to overtake you
once more

All the years spent lost in the wasted time
Fade away leaving us with a feeling that's numb
There's a part of you that wants to start anew
We're the "us" we've become
Throughout our lives time runs like a fuse
Whatever we've left behind has nothing to lose
We've found each other but still
As long as we hold back we go unfulfilled

I want to say right now
I want to be around
When you want
Your walls to come down
We will fill the spirit
And hear love's sound
Then we'll move
To a higher ground.

BEGINNINGS—HOLD ME CLOSE

Hold me close
Your arms make me so secure
I feel needed
I can endure

Hold me close
Your eyes speak to mine
In a language
They never thought they'd find

Hold me close
Your words reach my ears
As I listen
They help displace my fears

Hold me close
Your thoughts seem so clear
They open up mine
And draw me near

Hold me close
The passion that fills my heart
Speaks of a new beginning
A perfect start

Hold me close
Your heart beats out love
A perfect fit
A hand—a glove.

DESTINY

At a time of great destiny
Your whole life is composed by the will within you
Endlessly thinking—endless thoughts
These are moments of revelation

Where does the silence begin?
That's where I am found
At the beginning
Yet where the sun goes down

Be unashamed of your soul
The closeness lends enchantment to it's view
Is it any wonder we want time to stand still
As we listen in the stillness to the happiness

The sound of a harp can be heard
Can we remember the future?
Find a master drawing
This is the language of promise

Believe the feelings you hold near
While we leap toward our own deep mystery
Believe your heart
Submerge into the lingering chambers of love.

FINDING YOURSELF

If we allow ourselves we can be imprisoned in our past
This is a burden we may bear
Try to become the you that has been hidden
The journey has prepared us for a life we can share

Every moment is part of a larger meaning
We have shown ridiculous courage—not lack
Sitting down with reason
This separation has been a reunion of self with self . . .
Welcome back.

HOW LONG

How long must tomorrow wait?
Trying to rewrite your diary as dark anger blocks the way
Depths of darkness have filled your heart with poison
Loneliness is a place we don't have to stay

Vague promises can lead to destruction
If we allow ourselves to be imprisoned by our past
Lies and other crimes have made a deep impression
It's up to us how long we make it last

Ignoring troubles can't solve problems
After years of worn out apologies
Your reasoning has brought you to a crossroads
Let your sad memories go—reach your destiny

You see your hurt as a tortured dream
You have lived through this moment before
All things grow out of misfortune
Now—
    No more, no more.

The Observer

LISTEN

Far from your dungeon now
An attempt to develop a conscience came too late
Listen to your future
Timing is everything—you no longer must wait

Eternities spent in silence
But now the sun is rising calm and bright
The shouting can now be stacked in the attic
Fulfill your wishes in what is right

With courage to endure
Understanding comes slowly or so it seems
Consent to freedom by making the future a friend
Come with me—inside my dream.

MY EYES ONLY

Your eyes are closed
In the morning when I look your way
I try not to disturb the silence
That begins this wonderful day

In the beginning I was afraid to close my eyes
That it was just a dream
Afraid you would disappear
Maybe you weren't like you seemed

When you open your eyes
I hope you're happy with what you see
I will no longer try to become someone else
I'm nobody but me

I've done my best to open up
And let you see
What has been hidden behind walls
No one else sees this part of me

Much more than I could have hoped for
Our lives can grow
No longer fearing tomorrow
I just needed you to know.

The Observer

NIGHTMARE

And now begins a crumbling darkness
Such is madness that may be found
Suffering the intense depression
As the ceremony of innocence is drowned

The volcanic fires of yesterday are remembered
We hear the first rumblings of the earthquake
The pain of the past is too easy to recall
We did not know what was at stake

Half-remembered promises mean almost nothing now
Mercy, peace, love are not in place here
As innocence cries out for justice
The pain lends itself to longsuffering tears

It isn't supposed to be like this
Your smile in the mirror poorly hides sorrow
How long must you pay the bill of fear
For some there will be no tomorrow

Some scars can never be erased
As we remember things as we expected them to be
Silence and tears have been your sentence
Although that change was only evident to those who see

Like old lines to a bad song
Unbearable become the moments of dread
Fear and loathing can replace all thoughts
As the echoes of pain bounce inside your head.

RAIN

Today I faced the morning and it smiled
The rain was there
But it didn't seem to matter
I didn't have a care

When you smile
The sun shines in my heart
Especially when you're near
But even when we're apart

Rain hits the windshield
But I can see just fine
I rode the storm out
And found piece of mind.

SPECIAL

You find me special
I sometimes wonder why
Your feelings are important to me, too
You can see it in my eyes

What makes you want to be with me?
I'd really like to know
You help me feel warm all over
From my head down to my toe

You mean the world to me
I always want you near
I'll always be here for you
You'll never have to fear

You are so special—Thank you.

NO ONE ELSE

In the whole world
There could never be
Someone who'll love you
As much as me
Who'll constantly try
His best to do
As much for your happiness
As much for you
Who'll take the time
To treat you right
And give of myself
With all his might

I'm committed to us.

The Observer

FOR SO LONG

For so long
I've held the weight of the world
For so long
I thought I knew what happiness was
For so long
I've been a prisoner within myself
Thanks for helping me find myself.

TRUST IN OUR LOVE

Your loving kindness has helped me show
The me that only you can know
Now the only way that I can be
Is the way that only you can see

I trust in our love

It is so nice to share myself so
Totally the way only we can know
As we stay together I look forward to
Sharing many future memories with you

You can trust in our love.

DEEPER

Love gives me peace
It calms my day
Gives me direction
And lights my way
With a look and a smile
You let me know
There's a deeper side to me
It's okay to show.

TWO

It takes two people to fall in love
And two people can share one heart
When confusion seems to get in the way
The two of us can make our start
We can overcome problems
That seem to get in the way
And weather any storm we want
And never stray.

THOUGHTS OF YOU

Sometimes I'm surprised by the place
I close my eyes and think of your face
Into my thoughts you rush – in my mind
You are so beautiful, loving, and kind
Into my daydreams you constantly creep
Fully awake or deeply asleep
The vision of your happy smile
Follows me all the while.

As You Go

As you go
I miss you
I want you near
It is clear
We enjoy our time
Together sharing
Together caring
The time apart is too long
Too long in between
The good company
And happy eyes
My love grows ever stronger.

The Observer

TIME

Time
Is directly related
To the company you keep
When I'm with you
Time flies
Without you
It stands still
Is it any wonder
I want you near
Because I love you like I do.

TO ONE ANOTHER

We were drawn to one another
The very first day
Anticipating the future
In a very special way

Reaching out
For our first embrace
Pulling closer
Narrowing the space

The gap between us
Seemed far too wide
We wanted it bridged
Flowing with the tide

We wanted to give
Ourselves through our hearts
Always together
Nevermore to part

The comfort you brought me
The times that we shared
Began at that space in time
It began right there

And now, because you make me feel
Exactly as you do
I take this time to write these lines
And pledge my love to you.

The Observer

WE

For the times you let me be myself
For the times you understood my needs
For friendship, love, and happiness
We planted all the seeds

I want to dwell within you
As you dwell inside of me
To occupy a special place
Two "ones" would become "we."

The following are from my children:

HERO
Kimberly Taylor

He's a guitar player;
He never made it big
Like John Mayer,
But he likes to sing along
To every Dan Fogelberg song.

He has a strong mind,
Could have done anything
His heart desired.
Decided he was the teaching kind,
A mentor to younger minds.

He liked coaching sports teams.
He wasn't Bobby Knight or anything,
But he kept kids reaching
for their dreams;
That makes him a modern-day hero

Daddy, I love you
Daddy, I miss you
Daddy, I'm still your baby
Though I'm grown now
and out on my own.
You've always been there;
You've always shown you care,
And I know I never really said it before,
But your second to none.

He's been called an artist;
He sees it in his mind
And he draws it.
He's a kohl pencil etcher,
Quite the wooded landscape sketcher.

He's somewhat of a writer.
Wonder if he knows
Just what he inspires,
Exposing a piece of him
With just a piece of paper and pen.

He's been more than a father,
A Daddy to a son
And two daughters.
Sometimes we just make things harder,
But he never seems to mind.

Daddy, I love you.
Daddy, I miss you.
Daddy, I'm still your baby
Though I'm grown now
And out on my own.
You've always been there;
You've always shown you care.
I know I never really said it before,
But you're a hero.

The Observer

THE FATHER AND HIS CHILDREN

Jennifer Beckett

The Observer sits in solitude,
Lost within his thoughts.
He listens ever patiently,
Withholding shoulds and oughts.

He hears the drama queen play out
The woes about her day.
The kids, the man, deciding on a plan.
What *does* she need him to say?

The prophet is the quiet type,
His problems oft his own.
A prodigal son, the favored one.
He'll reap the seeds he's sown.

The lunatic with her projects,
Trying to find a name.
Too many goals, stick to one role.
He fears she'll lose her aim.

Observing means just watching,
Listening, but never involved.
Yet this man has been instrumental
In how their lives have evolved.

The Observer knows making judgments
May alienate those in his reach.

It is a fine line for a father
Between lecture and simply teach.

Though cautious, the man counts his blessings,
Thankful for the life he's had.
While his children, now grown, switch roles they have
known,
And begin to worry for Dad.

FROM THE PROPHET, TO FATHER WISDOM

Craig A. Toney

The Prophet remembered a long forgotten time
Happiness was dreamt of and singing could be heard
'Where did it all go?' he thought to himself with tears

I . Many Moons Ago

A son shining brightly through Mother's womb
A child, a boy . . . oh joy
Father Wisdom looked down to the child
Not knowing, the Prophet, his only son
Would never become the man
He had hoped the boy to be.

Later in life, Sunday Father and Son played on the radio
While sweet melodies of pitter pattering tear drops
Could be heard upon the Prophet's tainted, blackening
heart
This was the last time Father Wisdom would hurt him
Shadow puppets then danced on the walls
While not a soul was around
Quietly creeping down the dark halls
In the distance, a child's laughter was found

As a child the Prophet began to use crayons
And draw life the way he wanted it
As he got older, the crayons turned to pencil
And the pictures got even better
And even older still, as he watched the paint

Upon the canvas crust and dry
The Prophet realized that he had forgotten
To paint Father . . . into the picture

The Prophet ran as fast as the wind would carry him
And instead of chasing, Father cheered him on
This was the last time that he would make Father proud
He ran again as fast as the wind would carry him
And instead of cheering him on, Father Wisdom tried
to reach for him
He tried to shut the Prophet in to protect him
The Prophet only shut Father out to rejected him
The Prophet saw Father's hand and he ran faster . . .
and he ran harder
Held a grudge so damn tight
Squeezing and thinking that he just might
Create a diamond from things they couldn't take back
But the darkness had just began to fade to black

II. The Awakening

The Prophet had walked this path without
Father Wisdom
Many long days and many long nights
Lost to them, lost to himself
He broke south, spiraling down
Unbeknownst what was to come
His memories ware tainted
With the blood of many
They became his stepping stones
And he stepped on more than he'd like to admit
The crimson blood fell to the dusty dirt below

The Observer

103

Not because he forgot who Father was
But because he had forgot himself

Oh so sheltered he became
Trusting no one, even self
Lies, deceit and betrayal
Oh, how he longed to get out
Coming back to Father Wisdom just for a taste
Not for the wisdom. Not for the knowledge he
possessed
But the Prophet would always come back
When Father Wisdom had something he wanted.

The Prophet saw what he had done to many souls
And thought of those he had pained so many years ago
The weeds had grown over to strangle his lost dreams
But there was a light to pull him back through
He saw Father Wisdom in the distance
Reaching for him. Loving him.

The Prophet ripped and shredded
The weed entangled dreams
He wiped the webs from his eyes
And lies from his bloody tongue
And screamed aloud to the sky:
"You can't bring me down again . . . I am by far, not
finished yet!!!"
He stood and made an oath to self
"The path of the righteous
Is the one I walk upon
Nevermore shall I be lost
Or I'll be forever gone"

It took many years for the Prophet to forgive
Yet it only took a second for Father Wisdom to forgive
him . . .
 . . . every time. Over and over he would forgive . . .
unconditionally

III. Connection

The Prophet stared within the window of lost time
Seeking to find what was once his to grasp
To take back all of the harsh words
To bring about love and respect
Instead of hate and regret
But those times have long past
And because of their deeds, a shadow has been cast
He stares at the aging man through the window
And sees that it is but his own reflection

IV. So Good to See You Once Again

And the Prophet stood with Father Wisdom on top of
the knoll
At the edge of this beautifully untainted Garden
They surveyed the land that they'd created
The Prophet turned to Father Wisdom

"You know Father, I'm sorry for becoming who I
became."

Father Wisdom replied, "I've always loved you just the
same."

The Observer

The Prophet said, "I know you have and that's what hurts me the most."

Father replied, "There's no need to live with old ghosts.
I look back on your life son, and there are times when I'm not proud.
It saddens me when much of our communication, was shouting out loud.
But I am proud of you now, those times were baby steps to who you became.
I am honored to have you as a companion. Who cares who was to blame?"

With tears in his eyes, the Prophet wrapped his arms around Father Wisdom
"With time and age, and with hopes and dreams I strive
To be as you were and as you are . . . to be truly alive."

www.danielcraigtoney.com

www.ingramcontent.com/pod-product-compliance
Lightning Source LLC
Chambersburg PA
CBHW051818040426
42446CB00007B/725